CHERRYTREE BOOKS

THE LIVING PLANET

DESERTS

EDITED BY IAN JAMES

A Cherrytree Book

Adapted by A S Publishing from
Los Desiertos © Parramon Ediciones S.A. 1997
Editor: Rosa Fragua
Text: Nuria Roca
Illustrations: Antonio Muñoz
Design: Beatriz Seoane
Layout: Josep Guasch
Production: Rafael Marfil

This edition first published in 1998
by Cherrytree Press Ltd
a subsidiary of
The Chivers Company Ltd
Windsor Bridge Road
Bath BA2 3AX

© Cherrytree Press Ltd 1998

British Library Cataloguing in Publication Data
Deserts. – (The living planet)
1. Deserts – Juvenile literature
I. James, Ian
551.4'15

ISBN 0 7540 9030 2

Typeset by Dorchester Typesetting Group Ltd, Dorset
Printed in Spain

A bird's-eye view of a coastal desert.

CONTENTS

WHAT IS A DESERT?

DESERTS ARE PLACES with little rainfall. They make up about a fifth of the world's land area. To survive, desert animals and plants must be able to endure long droughts and hot weather. Scientists say that deserts are places with an average rainfall of less than 250 mm a year. But in some parts of the Sahara and Namib deserts in Africa, and also in the Atacama desert in South America, years may go by without a single drop of rain. Severe rainstorms sometimes occur, causing floods. But the rainwater soon disappears. It seeps into the ground or is evaporated by the hot sun.

Most deserts have dry and sunny climates. But some dry lands, such as the Gobi desert in central Asia, are bitterly cold, especially in winter. Some huge hot deserts lie to the north and south of the hot, rainy lands beside the equator. At the equator, the hot ground heats the air, which rises in strong currents. The rising air cools and then spreads out north and south. Around the tropics of Cancer and Capricorn, the air sinks back to the surface. This air becomes warmer and drier as it descends. The air presses down on the surface, producing dry winds that blow to the north and south. These winds stop moist winds reaching the land. As a result, rain is rare and the land is dry.

Other deserts are formed when winds lose most of their moisture as they blow over mountain ranges. On the far sides of coastal mountain ranges, the winds blow downhill, becoming warmer and drying the land. Dry winds also occur in the middle of continents. Deserts occur in these areas, because the winds lose their moisture in their long journey from the sea.

Hot deserts are found in five continents. The largest desert is the Sahara in North Africa. Asia and Australia also have huge deserts.

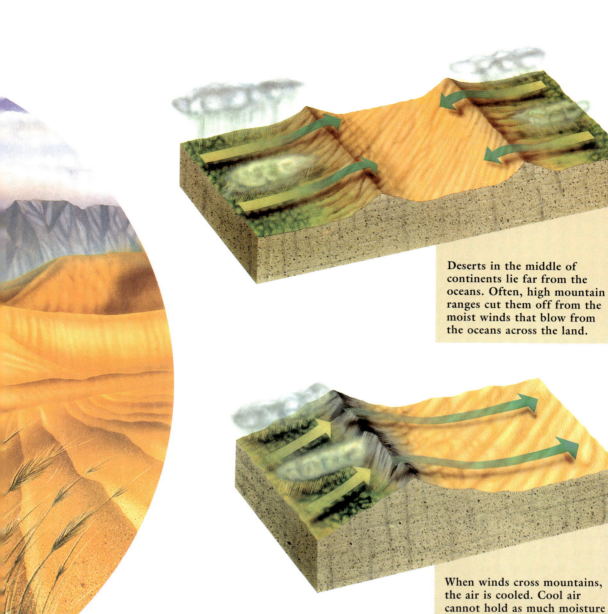

Deserts in the middle of continents lie far from the oceans. Often, high mountain ranges cut them off from the moist winds that blow from the oceans across the land.

When winds cross mountains, the air is cooled. Cool air cannot hold as much moisture as warm air, so moisture in the air condenses to form clouds.

Even when it rains in deserts, the water soon vanishes. Much of it is lost through evaporation, which occurs when heat from the sun turns water into an invisible gas called water vapour.

Some deserts, such as the Namib in Africa and the Atacama in South America, lie along coasts. They occur because the winds blowing from the sea are chilled by the cold seawater. When cool air from the sea blows across the land, the winds are warmed. Because warm air can hold more moisture than cool air, the winds keep their moisture.

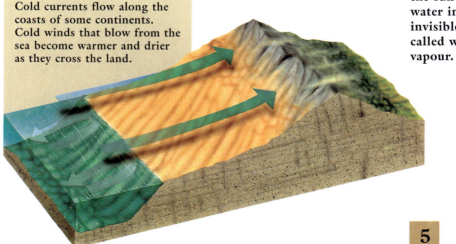

Cold currents flow along the coasts of some continents. Cold winds that blow from the sea become warmer and drier as they cross the land.

DESERT LANDSCAPES

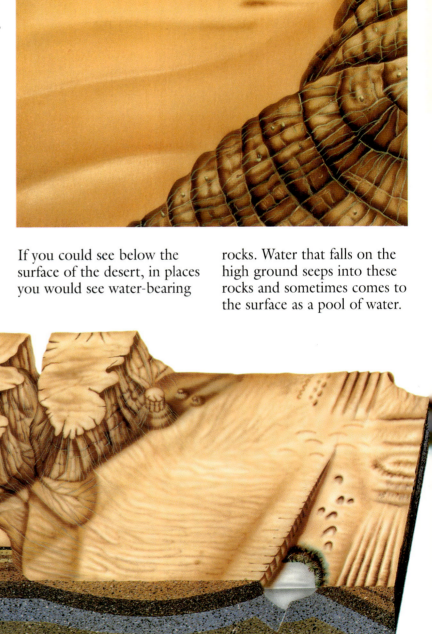

DESERTS CONTAIN much beautiful scenery, which strangely has been caused by water. During the millions of years of its history, the earth's climate has changed many times. Many areas that are now desert once had rivers flowing across them, or had plentiful rainfall. Water is able to wear away rock, and powerful rivers carve valleys which in time become deep canyons.

Monument Valley, right, in Utah in the United States was once a high plateau. A river and its tributaries wore away valleys, which became broader and broader as more land was carved by water or worn away by the wind. Today the only parts of the old plateau that remain are spectacular pillars of rock that have defied the forces of erosion.

If you could see below the surface of the desert, in places you would see water-bearing rocks. Water that falls on the high ground seeps into these rocks and sometimes comes to the surface as a pool of water.

Thousands of years ago, many deserts, including the Sahara, had rainy climates. The rain filled huge rivers that wore away deep valleys, which remain today even though they are dry.

On the surface you might see rocky hills and canyons, and plains covered by smaller rocks, or hills of sand called dunes. The forces of erosion that have created these features include temperature changes. Intense heat during the day makes the rocks expand. At night the desert may be cold and even frosty, right. The rocks shrink and crack, and may break up. Rocks are also worn away by wind-blown sand and by running water following rare storms.

Heavy rain creates torrents of water that wear out deep valleys. When the torrents from mountains reach flat plains, they often spread clay over the land. When the clay dries, it forms a surface like crazy paving, above.

Sometimes the water contains a lot of salt. When salty water evaporates, the salt is left behind and in time huge white salt flats are formed, above right.

Winds grind down the desert rocks and spread the sand, dust and gravel over the surface. Large areas of desert are covered by loose gravel with occasional plants.

ROCKY DESERTS

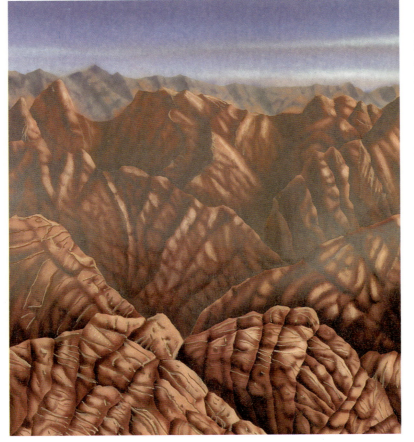

MANY PEOPLE think that sand covers the land in all deserts, but in fact most deserts are rocky. Some, called hammada, are bare rock, left. Others, called reg, are covered by loose gravel. In rocky deserts, the temperature of rocks often changes from 70°C by day to below freezing at night. These changes make rocks expand and contract until their surfaces crack, often making sounds like pistol shots. Cracking causes the outer layers of rocks to peel away. This process is called mechanical weathering.

Mushroom-shaped rocks, below, are formed when wind-blown sand wears away the bottom of a boulder, leaving the top part resting on a small stem. The wind cannot lift the heavy grains high enough to erode the top.

During freak storms, rainwater fills dried-up river valleys, called wadis. Torrents of water sweep away dust, sand and rock, making the wadi deeper and wider.

Some features were created when the climate was rainy, including flat-topped hills called mesas, above, and jagged pinnacles called buttes. These islands of hard rock remained while the surrounding soft rock was worn away. The bases of both formations are wider than the tops, because bits of weathered rock have piled up around them in heaps called scree.

Natural arches and rock bridges, right, are formed by water and wind. Water filters into an area of softer rock and loosens particles that are blown away by the wind, leaving tiny holes. Battered by the wind, these holes deepen until the rock is worn through and a large hole results, which becomes bigger and bigger.

Jagged buttes are the remains of mesas. They are striking landmarks in deserts. They are made of hard rocks that have resisted erosion.

9

SANDY DESERTS

SAND COVERS ONLY about a fifth of the world's hot desert. Sandy deserts, right, are called erg. Weathering, winds and running water break down rocks into smaller and smaller particles of sand and dust. Dunes, which are mounds or ridges of sand, form on rock surfaces when an obstacle, such as a plant or a small rock, lies in the path of the wind. Sand starts to pile up behind the plant or rock, creating a mound of sand, which eventually grows into a dune. The shapes of dunes vary. In places where winds blow from different directions, the dunes are often shapeless, although star-shaped dunes sometimes occur, right. Dunes are constantly on the move. Sometimes they bury towns and oases completely, below.

Winds in deserts continually blow the sand into dunes. Their shape depends on the wind direction and force.

Vast areas of dunes, such as those in the Sahara, above left, are often called sand seas. The long ridges of sand, left, which are parallel to the main direction of the wind, are like waves in the sea. Crescent-shaped dunes, called barchans, above right, form where the wind direction rarely changes. Winds blow sand up the gently sloping windward side of barchans, while grains of sand tumble down the steep leeward side.

Because of this constant movement, dunes creep forwards, often by 10 to 30 metres a year. The only way to stop them advancing is to plant grasses and other plants, above right. The plants anchor the sand and hold it in place. Few plants grow naturally in sandy deserts. Animals, like the gemsbok, left, that depend on plants or dew for moisture, keep to the edges of the desert where it is less dry.

Low ridges of sand form in areas where the wind blows mainly from the same direction. Larger dunes in the Sahara may reach heights of more than 450 metres.

THE WORLD'S DESERTS

Coastal deserts

Hot deserts

Deserts with cold winters

The sun's heat is most intense near the equator. Most areas around the equator are wet. Deserts lie north and south of these wet areas.

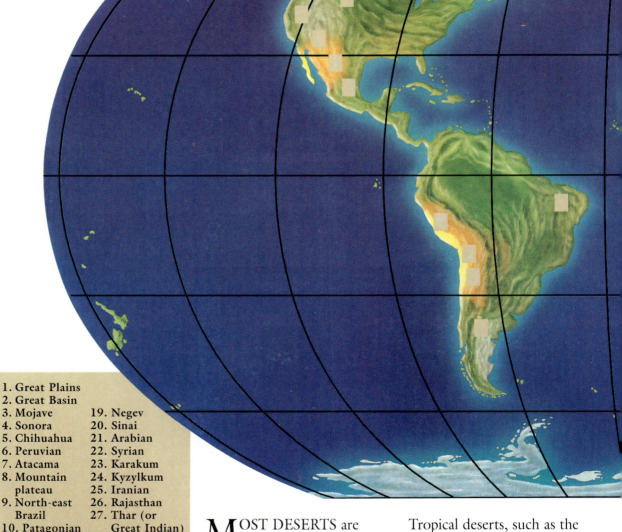

1. Great Plains
2. Great Basin
3. Mojave
4. Sonora
5. Chihuahua
6. Peruvian
7. Atacama
8. Mountain plateau
9. North-east Brazil
10. Patagonian
11. Sahel
12. Sahara
13. Western Desert
14. Nubian
15. Chalbi
16. Somali
17. Kalahari
18. Namib
19. Negev
20. Sinai
21. Arabian
22. Syrian
23. Karakum
24. Kyzylkum
25. Iranian
26. Rajasthan
27. Thar (or Great Indian)
28. Taklimakan
29. Gobi
30. Danikil
31. Great Sandy
32. Gibson
33. Great Victoria
34. Simpson
35. Sturt

MOST DESERTS are found around the tropic of Cancer (23.5° north of the equator) and the tropic of Capricorn (23.5° south of the equator). The region between these two imaginary lines, which are parallel to the equator, is called the tropics.

Tropical deserts, such as the vast Sahara and Arabian deserts, have high temperatures throughout the year, though nights can be cold. Both contain huge sand seas, where towering dunes reach great heights.

Coastal deserts, such as the Atacama, above, are cloudy and misty. They are less hostile to plants and animals than hot tropical deserts.

Cold deserts, such as the Gobi desert in China and Mongolia, lie outside the tropics. The Gobi desert lies on a high, windy plateau far from the sea. Temperatures in winter drop well below freezing point, but heat waves occur in summer.

Coastal deserts, such as the Namib in south-western Africa and the Atacama in Chile, lie on the tropic of Capricorn. Cold currents flow along the coasts of south-western Africa and Chile. Onshore winds are chilled by the cold water. The cool onshore winds keep down temperatures on land. Little rain falls in these areas, which are among the world's driest places. But some moisture for plants comes from dense mists that roll in from the sea.

WHEN RAIN DOES FALL

WHEN RAIN FALLS in the desert, plants and animals rush to make the best of it before it disappears. Cactuses and other succulent plants, right, are the most typical desert plants. They soak up water through their roots and use it during the long drought that follows.

All kinds of animals emerge from underground burrows to drink the rainwater. The spadefoot toad, below, which lives in the Sonora desert in North America, has more to do than drink. As soon as they hear the rain hitting the surface, the adult toads come out of their burrows and make for the deepest pools. They mate, and the females lay their eggs. When the eggs turn into tadpoles, there will still be enough water for them to swim in until they turn into toads.

When a flower blooms in the desert, it makes its seeds quickly. But the seeds may have to wait for years until there is enough rain for them to take root and grow.

The seeds of some plants lie dormant in the desert soil. When it rains, the seeds germinate: roots go down, shoots go up. Soon the desert is a carpet of flowers, right. At the same time, the eggs of insects hatch and turn into larvae. The full-grown insects then pollinate the flowers, enabling them to make seeds. The insects also mate, so that they can lay their eggs.

Other animals use the flowers and seeds to build up food stores. One kind of ant that lives in Mexico and the United States collects enough seeds to last for 12 years. Some Australian honey ants, below, store nectar in their abdomens, which swell up like grapes. The other ants in the nest feed on the store.

Desert animals use any source of water or food that they find. Certain kinds of butterflies, below right, get water and food from animal droppings.

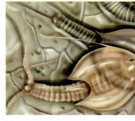

The eggs of these triops can survive in desert sands for ten years or more.

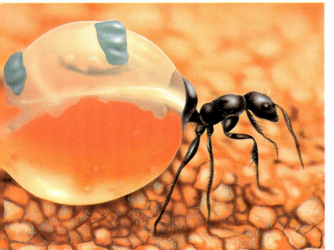

WATER IN DESERTS

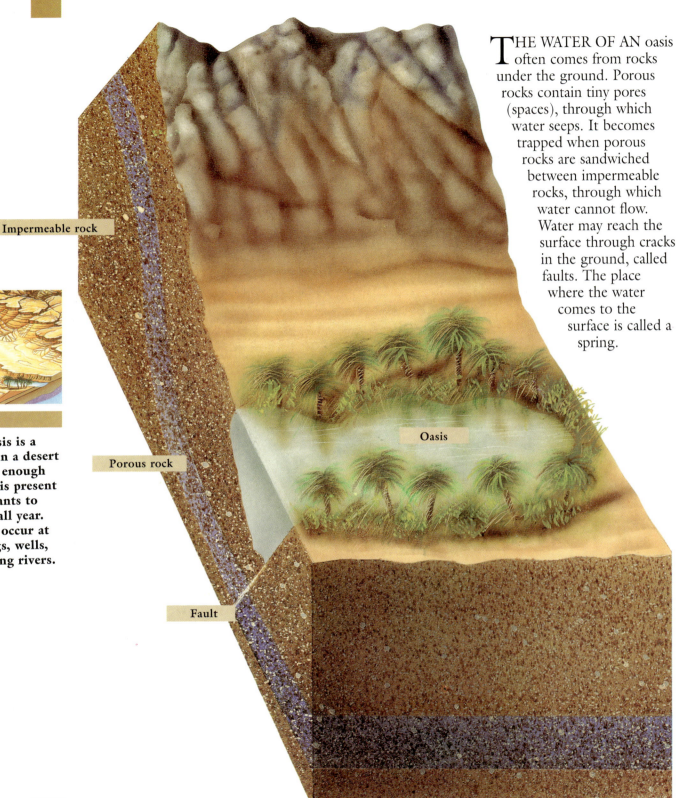

Impermeable rock

An oasis is a place in a desert where enough water is present for plants to grow all year. Oases occur at springs, wells, or along rivers.

Porous rock

Oasis

Fault

THE WATER OF AN oasis often comes from rocks under the ground. Porous rocks contain tiny pores (spaces), through which water seeps. It becomes trapped when porous rocks are sandwiched between impermeable rocks, through which water cannot flow. Water may reach the surface through cracks in the ground, called faults. The place where the water comes to the surface is called a spring.

Where there is no natural spring, people often dig a well down into the ground to reach the water. Without water from oases, few living things could travel far in the desert. Camels, above, are the best travellers. They can withstand heat and walk long distances without water. The camel stores fat, not water, in its hump. By the time it reaches an oasis, it is often thin and tired, and able to lap up more than a hundred litres of water.

River valleys in deserts are oases. The fertile strip along each bank of the river may vary in width from a few metres to several hundred. Egypt is a mainly desert country; most of its people live on the banks of the Nile, right. Other great rivers that bring water to deserts include the Euphrates in Iraq, the Indus in Pakistan and the Rio Grande and Colorado in North America.

Rivers come from streams that flow down mountains. They carry large amounts of fertile silt. When the rivers reach the lowlands, they often flood and spread silt over the land.

DESERT PLANTS

D ESPITE THE HARSH conditions, a wide variety of plants have special adaptations that enable them to live in deserts. Some are drought evaders, or ephemerals. They germinate and flower only after storms. Others, like the joshua tree, right, are drought resisters. They take in water when it is available, and do their best not to lose any. Some have long roots that seek underground water. Others have roots that spread out near the surface over a wide area, so that they can take advantage of floods.

Succulents, including cactuses, below, store water in their fleshy stems. These plants often have waxy or hairy surfaces to reduce loss of water through transpiration (the giving off of water vapour through pores, or stomata).

Others close their stomata during the day. To conserve water, many plants shed their leaves during droughts. Many have thorns to prevent animals eating them.

Desert plants either store water, or they have very long roots that can reach down to permanent underground water supplies. The roots of the mesquite, which grows in the south-western United States, may reach down 20 metres.

The best known desert plant is the saguaro cactus, right. Cactuses originated in North and South America, but they have been introduced to other parts of the world. The saguaro, which lives in the Sonora and other deserts of the south-western United States, is the largest cactus. It often reaches 15 or more metres high and can live up to 200 years. Like a tree, it provides homes, food and shade for birds and some other small creatures.

The welwitschia, below, grows in the Namib desert, and may live for 1,000 years. It has a long tap root, and a short woody trunk from which grows a single pair of leaves, up to a metre wide and two metres long. The leaves, which are torn to ribbons by wind-blown sand, absorb moisture from dew.

The deserts of the south-western United States have a rich vegetation of drought-resistant plants, many of which have spectacular flowers.

19

DESERT ANIMALS

The tracks of a sidewinder snake may be mistaken for wind-blown marks in the sand. Its sideways movement reduces its contact with hot sand.

YOU MIGHT EXPECT the desert to be an empty place, but in fact many animals make their home there. Through special adaptations of their bodies and their ways of life, they take advantage of the scarce food and water, and keep their enemies at bay. The moloch, or thorny devil,

above, is an Australian lizard. Its colouring helps it to merge into the rocky background and its spines make it look fierce, even though it is a peaceful anteater.

Many animals stay in cool nests or dens during the day. They emerge only at dusk when the temperature falls.

Some have special ways of cooling their bodies. The huge ears of the kit fox act like radiators, giving off heat. The big ears of the desert hedgehog serve the same purpose. The animals in the picture, below, do not all live in the same deserts.

1. Iguana
2. Rattlesnake
3. Kangaroo rat
4. Kit fox
5. Collared lizard
6. Skink
7. Roadrunner
8. Desert hedgehog
9. Sand grouse

Desert animals depend on plants or other animals for water. Some, such as coyotes, foxes and wild cats, get moisture from the bodies of their prey. Others, such as camels, go long distances without drinking. The sand grouse flies long distances to drink at oases. As it drinks, it soaks its feathers in the water and then flies back to its nest with them wet. It uses the moisture to cool the eggs. When the young hatch, they drink water from their parent's feathers.

Not all desert animals lead solitary lives. Meerkats, above, live in groups in dry areas in southern Africa. To make sure that predators do not attack them while feeding or get into the network of underground tunnels in which they live, they post guards as lookouts. When a predator approaches, the guards bark to warn the rest of the group.

Some desert beetles almost stand on their heads to drink on misty mornings. The mist collects on their backs and runs down to their mouths.

10. Coyote
11. Owl
12. Rattlesnake
13. Sidewinder
14. Jerboa
15. Ground squirrel
16. Desert tortoise

DESERT PEOPLE

SINCE ANCIENT times, people have found ways of living in deserts, but fewer and fewer of them now follow their traditional way of life. Many have settled in towns or villages beside the desert where they can find work, education and health care.

Some groups, including the San people of the Kalahari and the Aboriginal people of Australia, once lived as hunters and gatherers. They hunted wild animals and gathered berries, nuts and roots. With no settled homes and few possessions, they were always on the move.

Other nomadic peoples were herders who tended flocks of sheep, goats or camels. The animals provided them with meat, milk, cloth for their clothes and skins for

their homes, above. They, too, had to keep on the move searching for pasture and water. Desert nomads included the Tuareg of the Sahara, the

Bedouin of the Middle East and the Mongols of the Gobi. The Bedouin lived in communal tents, below, which they carried around with them.

People have lived in the desert for hundreds and thousands of years. Their deep knowledge enables them to survive the harsh conditions.

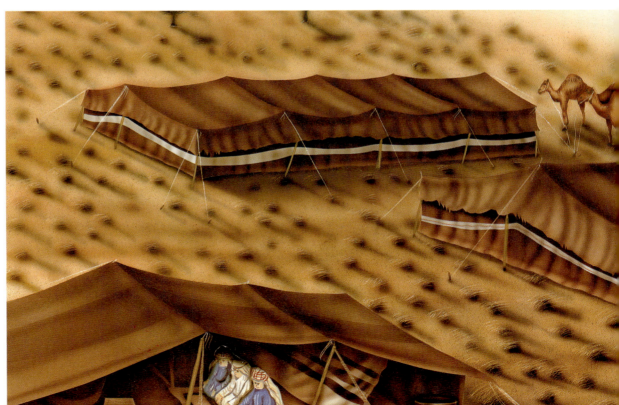

At oases, where there is a permanent water supply, people have built more settled homes. There is little wood available in deserts so buildings are made with stone or with sun-baked mud or clay, called adobe. The mud is mixed with straw to make bricks. Whole towns are made of this baked clay with buildings several storeys high. They have thick walls and small windows and doors, often facing into an inner courtyard, right. This protects them from the heat of the sun and the cool of the night, and from sandstorms.

The Dogon people of Mali are farmers. Once they built villages of adobe, below right. The houses had flat roofs to collect water from storms, and there were granaries with thatched roofs, in which they stored millet, maize and other grains.

The Mongols of the Gobi desert still make tents, called yurts, of many layers of skins and felt tied over a wooden frame.

SPREADING DESERTS

IN RECENT YEARS, the world's deserts have been spreading. During droughts, many deserts become larger. The areas where land has been turned into desert are dry grasslands, such as the Sahel, south of the Sahara. In years when rain is plentiful, the people in the Sahel plant crops and graze the land with their goats and sheep, below. They also cut down trees and shrubs for firewood. When droughts occur, the crops fail and the soil is exposed to sun and wind. The starving animals strip the trees of their leaves, so that they too die, above. The dry soil breaks up into fine dust which is blown away by the wind, leaving the land infertile. This process is called desertification.

In the 1930s, droughts occurred in parts of the United States. Farm crops failed and cattle grazed the pastures bare. Strong winds blew away the dry soil, creating a desert-like area called the Dust Bowl.

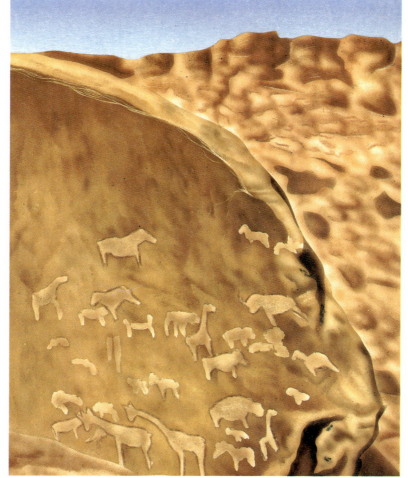

In some places, where only bare rock remains, desertification may be permanent. But elsewhere the land recovers, and when the rains return, grasses and other plants start to grow again, above.

Thus deserts come and go, as climates change and continents drift. Hippopotamus fossils and cave paintings of animals, right, found in the Sahara are evidence that thousands of years ago the area was covered with lush vegetation. Rock and cave paintings also show people hunting animals, as well as herding cattle. Then, around 5000 years ago, the Sahara began to dry up. Rivers and lakes disappeared, grasses shrivelled and trees died. Most people moved to areas with water, such as the Nile valley.

When deserts advance, people and animals starve. They are forced to leave their land and seek food and help in towns and camps.

SUN AND WIND

DESERTS APPEAR to be barren places, but they have many resources. Some, like the sun and the winds that provide currents for hot-air balloons, right, are obvious. Others are hidden. Vast amounts of oil and natural gas are found beneath the ground. Saudi Arabia, a desert country in the Middle East, is the world's leading oil exporter. The oil and gas are used as fuel for motor cars, for industry and for making electricity. Other desert countries that produce oil include Algeria and Libya in North Africa, and Iran, Iraq, Kuwait and the United Arab Emirates in the Middle East. Most desert people still rear cattle or raise crops, below, to make a living. They are poor compared with the people who run, or work in, the vast oil industry.

Some deserts contain other valuable minerals. Australia's deserts contain gold, iron ore, opals and uranium.

Water found in rocks beneath the ground is another important resource. The water is pumped to the surface and carried through pipelines to irrigate crops. Harvests are usually abundant on irrigated land in deserts, because plants grow well with plenty of water and sunshine. But water from the rocks is not being renewed. The wells that tap it will eventually dry up, as will the oil wells. For this reason, people are trying to make better use of renewable resources.

A bird's-eye view of three circular desert fields. They are made green by rows of rotating sprinklers that use water pumped up from water-bearing rocks below ground.

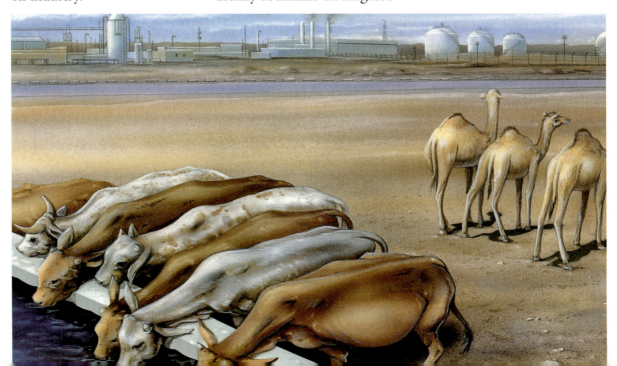

The supply of sun and wind in the desert is inexhaustible. Both can be used to produce electricity. In some areas, solar furnaces, above, are already in use. The sun's rays heat solar panels, which heat water and produce steam, which drives machines called turbines that produce electricity. In places where the winds are constant, they drive windmills, right, that produce electricity.

Electricity can be used to remove salt from seawater, making it fresh and usable by farmers. This process, called desalination, is expensive and only the richer countries can afford it.

Many people visit deserts to see and experience their magnificence. These tourists are a good source of income, but they also bring problems, upsetting the delicate balance of nature. Without care, damage can be done to the land and all its inhabitants.

Water is a precious resource in deserts. Sprinklers used to turn the dry land into fertile fields are turned on at night, so that as little water as possible will evaporate.

27

UNDERSTANDING DESERTS

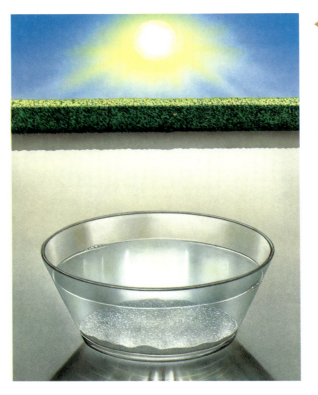

SALT FLATS

Salt is used to preserve food and add flavour to it. In ancient times it was very valuable, and desert peoples traded salt for goods they needed. Many deserts contain salt flats. These are dried up lakes. The lakes contain water only after heavy rain, and the water is salty, because it contains particles of salt that the water has washed from the rocks. The fierce heat of the sun evaporates the water very quickly and the lake disappears, leaving only a layer of salt on the ground. The next time the depression is flooded, more salt is deposited. In this way, the layer of salt gets thicker and thicker as time goes by.

You can see how this happens by carrying out a simple experiment. Dissolve ten teaspoons of salt in half a litre of water. Pour the water into a shallow bowl and leave it in direct sunlight. When the water has evaporated, you will see a layer of salt on the bottom of the bowl. Repeat this several more times and you will see how the layer of salt thickens.

FROST ACTION

In some parts of the desert, night-time temperatures may fall below freezing point in winter. The frost that forms causes weathering of the rocks, an action so powerful that it can split rocks apart. Water freezes in cracks in rocks, and because ice occupies nine per cent more space than the same volume of water, it pushes against both sides of the cracks, widening them and, eventually, splitting the rocks apart.

You can see how this happens with a slab of damp clay. Use a blunt knife to cut some cracks in one side of the slab. Then fill the cracks with water, wrap the slab in a plastic bag, and put it in the freezer. After a few hours, or next day, put the slab out in the sun to dry. Then water the cracks again and refreeze it. Keep doing this until your slab breaks up.

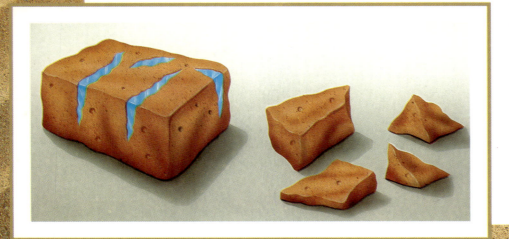

MIRAGES

Thirsty desert travellers sometimes think that they can see an immense lake ahead of them, and find to their disappointment that the oasis recedes as they approach it. The lake is an optical illusion called a mirage. Mirages occur because rays of light are refracted, or bent, as they pass through layers of air of different temperatures. This causes the observer to see two views, the real one and an inverted image of the real one. The blue colour of a lake mirage is a reflection of the sky, while the ripples in the 'water' are caused by the heat. You can photograph mirages. In the diagram light reaching the man's eye along the curved line makes him see an inverted tree.

USING A COMPASS

Finding your way across deserts is difficult unless you have a compass. The compass shows where north is. To make a simple compass, you need a magnet, a needle, a cork and a glass of water. Stroke the needle several times in the same direction with one end of the magnet. This magnetises the needle. Place the needle on the cork and let the cork float in the water. The needle will always point north/south.

GLOSSARY

ABDOMEN Part of an animal's body that contains its stomach.

ABORIGINAL PEOPLE People who are descended from the original people of a region or country.

ADAPTATION Ways in which animals and plants have evolved to better suit their surroundings.

ADOBE Sun-dried clay or mud brick.

BALANCE OF NATURE Natural state in which plants and animals live and interact with each other without seriously altering the make-up of the environment.

BARCHAN A crescent-shaped sand dune.

BUTTE A small mesa formed where a layer of hard rock at the top protects weaker rocks below.

CACTUS A succulent plant that stores water in its thick, fleshy stem. Most cactuses have spines.

CANYON A deep valley.

CONDENSE/CONDENSATION When a gas (such as water vapour) turns to liquid (water), it condenses.

CURRENTS Distinctive flows of air in the atmosphere or water in the oceans.

DESALINATION The removal of salt from seawater or other salty water, making it suitable for human consumption or for farming.

DESERTIFICATION The natural or human processes involved when a dry or fertile region is turned into desert.

DEW Moisture formed on objects on the earth's surface when water vapour condenses into tiny water droplets.

DORMANT Inactive, as if sleeping.

DROUGHT A long period with little or no rain.

DROUGHT EVADERS Plants or animals that are dormant during droughts, but spring into life when it rains.

DROUGHT RESISTERS Plants or animals that have special adaptations to conserve water during droughts.

DUNES Piles of sand created in deserts and along coasts by the wind.

EPHEMERALS Plants that live only for a short time.

EQUATOR An imaginary line around the centre of the earth.

ERG Sandy desert.

EROSION The wearing away of the land by weathering, running water, ice and winds.

EVAPORATE/EVAPORATION When a liquid (such as water) turns into a gas (water vapour), it evaporates.

FAULT A break in a layer of rock.

FELT A fabric formed without weaving from wool fibres and hairs.

GERMINATE To begin to grow.

GRAVEL Small rounded stones.

HAMMADA Areas of bare rock in deserts.

IMPERMEABLE ROCK A rock layer through which water cannot seep.

INFERTILE Unproductive.

IRRIGATION Watering the land by artificial means.

LARVA/LARVAE Immature animal or animals in a state quite different from that of the adult. Caterpillars are larvae.

LEEWARD Side of a mountain or other object that is sheltered from the wind.

MECHANICAL WEATHERING The breaking up of rocks caused by changes in temperature.

MESA A flat-topped upland, bounded by steep sides.

MIRAGE Optical illusion often seen in deserts.

MIST Thin cloud at ground level.

NATURAL ARCH An arch or bridge of rock formed by natural processes.

NATURAL GAS A fuel, formed from the remains of once-living organisms, found in the rocks in the earth's crust.

NOMAD A person who moves around with no permanent home.

OASIS Area of green in a desert where a spring, well or river provides a permanent water supply.

OIL A fuel found in the rocks in the earth's crust, formed from the remains of once-living organisms; it is also called petroleum.

PASTURE Fields of grass on which sheep and cattle can graze.

PLATEAU A high area where the land is generally level.

POLLINATION occurs when pollen from the male part of a flower combines with the female part of (usually) another flower and fertilizes it.

POROUS ROCK A rock, such as sandstone, which contains tiny pores which can absorb water.

REFRACTION The way rays of light appear to 'break' when they travel through water, air or glass.

REG Area of desert covered by loose gravel.

RENEWABLE RESOURCES Sources of energy, such as sun, wind and water, that cannot be used up.

SAGUARO Giant branched cactus that grows in American deserts.

SALT Substance dissolved in seawater, and in some desert lakes, that is used to preserve and flavour food.

SALT FLATS Areas of land where water evaporates and leaves a layer of salt.

SAN The people of the Kalahari desert, once known as Bushmen.

SAND Particles of rock that are finer than gravel, but coarser than dust.

SCREE Mass of weathered rocks of all sizes that pile up in heaps at the bottom of cliffs or mountain slopes.

SILT Sediment carried by a river and deposited over the land by floods or at the river's mouth.

SOLAR FURNACE Assembly of reflective panels that capture the heat of the sun and use it to make electricity.

SPRING A flow of water from the ground on to the surface.

STOMA/STOMATA A hole or holes through which a plant gives off water: usually in leaves.

SUCCULENTS Large group of drought-resistant plants that have fleshy leaves and/or stems. Cactuses are succulents.

TRANSPIRATION The giving off of water by the leaves of a plant.

TRIBUTARIES Small rivers that flow into bigger ones.

TROPICS The region between the tropic of Cancer and the tropic of Capricorn, two imaginary lines north and south of the equator. It is the world's hottest zone.

VALLEY Low stretch of land, usually formed by a river.

WADI A valley in a desert that is usually dry and contains water only after a rare rainstorm.

WEATHERING Mechanical or chemical processes that break up rocks.

WELL A deep hole, or shaft, dug in the ground to reach oil or water below.

WIND A current of air.

WINDWARD The side of a mountain or other object that faces into the wind.

YURT The traditional tents of the Mongol people of the Gobi desert.

INDEX

Numbers in italic refer to illustrations